77 Ways to Get More Customers

By Chris Cardell

First Edition published 2019

Printed and bound in Great Britain
www.ElitePublishingAcademy.com

A catalogue record for this book is available from The British Library

ISBN 978-1-912713-88-2

For more strategies, tips and tools on how to grow your business and get more customers, go to www.ChrisCardell.com for your £500 worth of FREE business building bonuses.

Table of Contents

77 Ways to Get More Customers

Although you and I may not have met yet, I know enough about you as an Entrepreneur, willing to read this book, to predict why you decided to set up your own business in the first place.

You did it for one reason:

FREEDOM.

Whether it's the freedom to work for yourself and never have to be an employee again, or to achieve financial freedom for you and the people you care about, I believe that the Entrepreneurial pursuit of freedom is one of the noblest there is.

Most people just dream of financial freedom.

You took action and actually did something about it. Congratulations!

But as a business owner, there is only one way to achieve that financial freedom – and that is the acquisition of customers.

Getting customers is the biggest problem in business. It's also the area that business owners struggle with the most. We spend so much time perfecting our product or service, only to realise that this means nothing if we don't somehow become amazing at getting customers. This can be daunting.

The good news is, once you realise that the business you are really in is the 'getting customers' business, and you decide to get very good at it, you are virtually guaranteed financial freedom.

This book is about solving the 'getting customers' problem for you and helping you achieve that financial freedom – fast.

I've spent the last 20 years helping business owners across the world increase their profits by 50% to 250% by becoming very, very good at getting customers. (You can find out more about me at **www.ChrisCardell.com**) I grew my reputation and got all the media coverage because in those two decades I've achieved these breakthroughs for Entrepreneurs much faster than most people think is possible.

It's important to know that the strategies you are about to read are not theories. They are based on what's working right now. I've got to know many millionaire Entrepreneurs over the years. They are doing some or all of what's in this book. The other 99% of business owners aren't, it's as simple as that.

I've left out the very obvious stuff like 'have a great website', because I'm assuming you know that! I've focused on some of the more advanced strategies, along with more fundamental ones. I want you to be able to grow your business regardless of what's going on in the economy. One of the nice bonuses is that this will recession-proof you and your business beyond your wildest expectations.

Talking of bonuses, be sure to claim your £500 of Free bonuses, including my Online Video programme '7 Website Game Changers' which shows you everything you need for a successful website and online marketing.

You can claim your Free bonuses at:

www.ChrisCardell.com

Now, let's get straight into to our 77 ways to attract customers into your business.

Strategy 1: Unconverted Leads

If I came into your business today, what's the very first thing I would do to get more customers into your business? I would focus on the unconverted leads. I promise that you have gold sitting in your business in what's known as your unconverted leads.

If you say to most business owners, "How are you going to get more customers?" they will normally start talking about new or additional forms of marketing and advertising. They'll say, "I'll advertise in the newspaper or do some pay-per-click on Google. I'll exhibit at tradeshows." That's great, but that's not the first thing you want to do. That's not the lowest-hanging fruit when it comes to getting new customers.

Between your existing customers and the people who've never heard from you that you want to reach with effective marketing, there's another group that everybody ignores. It's insane. In marketing, they are what we call your unconverted leads. An unconverted lead is somebody who has phoned you, emailed you, come into your premises, or made some kind of contact with you and expressed interest in what you have to offer, but they have not followed through and bought, for whatever reason.

The big mistake people make is assuming that because somebody doesn't buy from you today, this week, or this month, they're never going to buy from you. That's a terrible mistake. You know what it's like to buy. You inquire about products and services, don't you? Do you always act straight away, or does it sometimes happen weeks or months down the line?

Unconverted leads are not lost customers. Your marketing needs to include these leads, and this can be done through a variety of tried-and-tested methods.

Strategy 2: Multiple Follow-up

Focusing on those unconverted leads is crucial for any business. They should be number one on the list. Work those leads until they buy, die, or tell you to go away. The principle way to do that is with multiple follow-up, because most businesses give up far too easily.

Let's say somebody emails or phones you about what you have to offer, and you have a record of who they are. Most people will reply to the email or phone the person up, and maybe they'll send something in the post or send an email with additional information attached. In other words, they'll follow up with that customer once or twice. That is what 90 per cent of businesses do.

There have been so many interesting studies on this, it's been researched again and again. On average, if you do multiple follow-ups properly, it takes seven points of contact to convert a lead, a potential customer who has inquired with you, into a buying customer.

The form of contact is going to vary slightly depending on the business you're in, but the principle is always the same. On average, your customer is going to need an email, another email, maybe a phone call, maybe another email, maybe something in the post, maybe a face-to-face meeting if it's appropriate for you, maybe another email or two, and only then do they become a customer.

I ask a question at our Entrepreneur Summit, and the answer never fails to amaze me. I ask, "Who's been on my email list for three years, and this is the first time you've actually spent any money with me?" Every year, there are 30, 40, and sometimes 50 people who raise their hand. If they've been on my email list for three years, they've probably had 150 to 200 emails from me. Most businesses and entrepreneurs give up at just one or two.

You absolutely need to do multiple follow-ups. If somebody comes within a mile of your business, you want to have a system in place for this, whether it be email, direct mail, telephone calls, or other forms of good marketing. We're going to touch on some of those other forms of marketing as we go through our 77 steps. As a basic principle though, you've got to have a strong multiple follow-up system in place and be communicating with people again and again.

Strategy 3: Referrals

Next is getting your existing customers to give you your new customers. Before you spend any marketing and advertising money, you should encourage your customers to give you new customers for free, through referrals.

Pretty much everybody gets referrals. A lot of businesses actually exist on them. Almost without exception, the referrals are accidental. In other words, they sort of happen by accident because the business owner does nothing to get them, other than providing a good product or service to the customers they have. They are in no way being proactive in getting referrals.

You want to be proactive about this. You want to have a system in place. The absolute first thing you want to do is have a referral culture in your business. A referral culture involves your customers understanding that referrals are a core part of how you grow and that they, as your customer and as part of the relationship, almost have a requirement to give you referrals.

That might sound a bit strong, but you can do this effectively, build it into the system, and have a dialogue with the customer when they first become a customer of yours. You can say, "I build my business primarily through word-of-mouth recommendation with individuals like yourself. If I do a great job for you, would you be willing to recommend me to friends, family, and colleagues?" Who's going to say no to that?

The interesting thing is just putting that concept in people's heads, literally implanting that idea in their mind, will increase referrals on its own. If every customer that became a customer of yours next week brought one person into your business, and then that person brought one more person into your business, you'd never have to do any marketing or advertising again. That is the sheer power of referrals.

Strategy 4: Supplier Referrals

There are some more advanced things around referrals that for some reason, people tend to overlook. For example, you want to get supplier referrals. Obviously, you want to get customer referrals, but you also want to find out who your suppliers might know who could also be potential customers of yours. Establish a good relationship with your suppliers if you haven't already, ask the question, and get the contact details of all those untapped potential customers. If you put the initial time in, this is a brilliant way to increase your customer-base, without having to spend a single penny.

Strategy 5: Referral Marketing Campaigns

People generally accept that they should have marketing campaigns in their business, meaning you promote a specific product or service, and you have a marketing campaign that consists of things you send through the mail, emails, a website, and a specific web page you set up for it. You may even call or go to see your customers about it. That's a marketing campaign in a nutshell.

Importantly, you also need a marketing campaign purely for referrals. Referral customers are the best customers for two reasons. First, they're free to get. Second, they're better customers. They will normally spend more money and be better behaved because there's an initial relationship that brings them there.

Send your existing customers to a page on your website asking for referrals. Perhaps offer rewards, bonuses, or vouchers if they give you a referral. Why wouldn't you send emails to your customers two or three times a year asking for this? You can send a letter to your 100 best customers for somewhere between 50 and 100 pounds or dollars. Why wouldn't you do that a couple of times a year if that brought in three, six, or 19 new customers? You want to have a referral marketing campaign just like you want to have any other marketing campaign.

Strategy 6: Improve Sales Skills

What I would really like you to achieve is for you to have an all-round understanding of the art and science of getting customers. I could just rattle off very specific strategies. For example, "do this on the second page of your website". However, if you really want to become superb at getting customers, you really must understand and be able to practise the art of it, the slightly intangible element of sales.

Your ability to sell effectively is as important to your ability to get customers as anything else, and it always will be. If you have a team around you, the same obviously applies for your team.

I highlight this because most business owners don't go into business to sell. They don't think, "I'd like to leave this lousy job I'm in and spend all day selling things to people," because most people don't particularly like the idea of selling. You normally go into business because you really want to get out of the job you're in, or you're really motivated to carry out a service or offer a particular product. Which is great, however, as I'm sure you've realised by now, this is nowhere near enough to be successful. Everything in your business success boils down to just two things. Sales and marketing.

Whether you're growing a huge company or starting a little business from your back bedroom, you are an entrepreneur. As an entrepreneur you have to get great at selling, not just so you yourself can sell, but so that you can also make sure the key people on your team are also doing it well.

There are all sorts of ways to improve your sales skills. You can take courses, read books and attend seminars, but my core message to you is that you need to understand the fundamental importance of sales as part of the customer attraction and acquisition strategy within your business.

George Foreman, the two-time world heavyweight champion, Olympic gold medallist, and entrepreneur, said that if he could teach his children one thing in life, it would be to sell. Once you can sell, you will never lose your home or be short of money because people always want great salespeople. As a business owner, you already know this. Wouldn't you love three great salespeople to walk in the door tomorrow? This is one of life's most important skills, so improve your sales skills in whichever way you can.

Strategy 7: Overcome Objections

This is an area people tend not to focus on, and yet it's so incredibly important. Business owners tend to focus on "I want more customers. Where am I going to place the advert for maximum exposure?" Yes, that's important, but once you have their attention, you also need to look at any objections to the sale.

Let's turn the tables and think of it like this: What's stopping you getting more customers? I've already touched on leads, and about people inquiring. Every business has a conversion rate, which is the percentage of people who contact you and become customers. A percentage of people who visit your website, walk onto your premises, or phone you up have the potential to become customers, but it's never 100 per cent. It could be anything from 1 per cent to 60 per cent, depending on who you are, where you are, and what you're doing. It's normally way under 50 per cent.

Understand that if you've paid for your marketing and advertising to bring that person close to becoming a customer, the cost is already there for you. So if you can increase that conversion percentage, that's a very effective use of your time.

Why would somebody go to the trouble of inquiring about your business, filling in a form on your website, or picking up the phone to call you and then not buy? They're obviously interested in what you're selling. Assuming what you have is of good value and meets their needs, why wouldn't the figure be 100 per cent?

The answer is customer objections. The thing that stops a sale happening is rarely that you don't have what a customer needs or wants. Obviously, if you don't have what they need or want, you let them go, but that's not normally what's going on. Normally, there's an objection in your customer's head.

Some of the big objections are money and time. "It's too expensive," is a big objection. "I don't have time to invest in doing this," would be another objection. You're also going to have objections specific to your business.

If you pay attention to what your customers tell you, you – and your colleagues if you work in a larger business – should become very clear on what your customers' objections are.

Literally list them one by one and, between you, work out smart answers to those objections. There will only be three or four objections you hear all the time, and you can get really good at answering those.

One of the big objections I hear from business owners is "I haven't got time to do this. I'm busy." I have an answer to that; if you're a business owner who's not willing and able to spend three out of 365 days a year immersed in the leading-edge, latest internet marketing because you're too busy, you have big problems." There's a reframe or an answer to nearly every objection.

Strategy 8: Ask for The Sale

Another thing in the sales process is going to sound ridiculously obvious, but it's important. You must ask for the sale. It's a tragedy how many salespeople, but also business owners generally, do everything well when they communicate to a customer – they present what they have, answer questions, and even sometimes overcome objections well – but when it comes to that key moment to say, "Should we confirm the order now?" or "How would you like to pay?" they don't say it. Maybe they have some psychological hang-ups in place. You must ask for the sale, and you must make sure your team asks for the sale.

There can be many people involved in your business, whether they're salespeople or the receptionist. If you think the receptionist who answers your phone isn't a salesperson involved in the sales process, you'll want to think again. Anybody involved in the sales process needs to be awarded and compensated in a way that is linked to the sales.

Fifteen years ago, I went into companies to talk about influence and sales skills to sales teams. It shocked me how many sales teams were on a flat salary. There was no commission involved. Sales managers would say, "We have doughnuts on Friday at the team meeting." If they're having doughnuts anyway, then on a cold, wet Wednesday afternoon when they have to make an extra call or go into a business to ask for the sale, they're not going to do it if they're not compensated. That's really important.

Strategy 9: Send More Emails

Let's jump to the internet briefly and talk about email. If you want more customers, send more emails. Nobody is sending enough emails. You want to send at least one email a week to your customers, if not more. Ideally, you want to have a relationship with them where you can send more because not every single email you send is a sales marketing email. Some are just adding value by giving useful information. According to a 2018 study, there will be more than 3.8 billion email users world-wide by 2019, over 100 million more than the previous year. So not only is email use increasing rapidly year-on-year and is many people's preferred way of communication, it enables businesses to tap into customers around the country, around the world, and at no financial cost to you and your business. And, perhaps more importantly, your email subscribers have already explicitly told you they want to hear from you by giving you their email address. Capitalise on that. Send more email.

Strategy 10: Make Sure Your Emails Are Opened

If you want to get more customers, you need to send more emails, but there's no point in sending them if your customers are not opening them. If you look at open rates in email delivery, they are somewhat shocking. They can be as low as 10 or 12 per cent.

How do you get your emails opened? You do that with the title of your email. The title of your email is the most important part of your email. It's like a headline in a newspaper ad. It determines whether they're going to read the rest of the email.

If you look down your inbox at the emails you get from businesses, they tend to be unbelievably boring titles, and that's why so many business emails aren't opened. "A 10 per cent price saving" is not an exciting email title.

If you look at the titles of the emails I send, they are hopefully either interesting, intriguing, funny, or controversial. I'll do whatever it takes it to get people to read the email. When an email comes into your inbox, you're going to be selective about the ones you open, so you must use creative titles in your email.

Strategy 11: Test A Daily Email Service

I'm not saying to send your customers daily emails from day 1, although a lot of people use that strategy very effectively. If you don't want to do that, at least give them the option of receiving a daily email, like a daily email tip or a thought for the day. I'll bet there are 365 ideas, thoughts, insights, reflections, or funny stories that you have on the business you're in.

They can be one- or two-line emails, and they don't have to be about business. If you see a great film Wednesday night, your email on Thursday morning to everyone could say, "Hi. Chris here. I saw a great film last night. Al Pacino is brilliant. You've got to see this. Talk to you tomorrow." Bang.

You might say, "What does that have to do with business or selling?" It creates or reinforces a relationship. On new customer acquisition and converting those leads, this can have a big impact.

Strategy 12: Use Direct Mail

Going on for over 100 years now, direct mail has been an incredible way of getting customers into any business, but it's not used by small businesses anything like as much as it should be.

Everyone is excited about the internet, and I'm generally well-known for the internet material I do. I'm a raving fan of the internet as much as anybody else, but if direct mail is still an equally valid source of new business and new customers for you, why wouldn't you use it?

The challenge of getting somebody who doesn't know you and who's never spent money with you to give you money is a significant one. A lot of that can be done on the internet, but there is a big proportion of the population who still value and want something physical to look at, understand, and literally hold in their hands before they give you money.

This applies more as your price point goes up. If you're selling for £4.95, it's much easier to do it online. Once you get past 100 or 200 pounds or dollars, you're into a different ball game where the use of direct mail is very effective.

If you look at what comes through your letterbox in your home or business life, you'll see a lot of stuff. Direct mail isn't cheap, but people do it because it works.

The beauty of direct mail is that it's so personal. How else can you get right in front of people having a direct conversation with them, saying whatever you need to say to them, in their kitchen or as they sit in the garden? Use direct mail.

We're focusing here on getting new customers, but the nice thing is you can use this for your existing customers too. It has to be said that it's easier to get your existing customers to spend money with you through any form of marketing, including direct mail. You definitely want to do it with existing customers, but I really hope you'll try this out with new customers as well.

Strategy 13: Personalise Your Mailings

Always hand-address your envelopes or at least use a handwriting font. Try to avoid labels or fonts that look anonymous and cold.

The same obstacles surrounding people opening emails, also apply to direct mail. We want to do direct mail, but one of the biggest challenges is getting people to open your mailing to read it and not just throw it in the bin or leave it around and ignore it.

Don't assume that if you send 100 mail pieces, that 100 people are going to read it. Unfortunately, that's not how it works. We need to have as many people as possible read the thing in the first place. That's going to stack the deck in your favour. To do that, you obviously need to get your envelope opened.

The more personal it is, the more likely they are to open it. We've done tests in our business. This isn't a universal rule because it will vary, but we've found that if we put a physical stamp on the letter, it will double our response for new customer acquisition. The only reason it can be is it gives the impression of a more personal letter, so they open it and read it. A printed postage stamp is a pretty good indication this is coming from a business, and it can probably wait. Then they'll likely never get around to opening it.

Strategy 14: Test Teaser Copy

Test teaser copy on the outside of the envelope. Again, you'll see this on the mailings you get from big companies. Why don't small businesses do this? This is copy on the envelope, words that encourage and entice people to read. It could be a couple of sentences or just one word. It could simply say "private", "private and confidential", "top secret", or something similar to increase intrigue, and therefore, readership.

If you look at the copy on the envelopes from bigger companies, it's the credit card companies and people like that who tend to use teaser copy, but a lot of the copy is not very good. It's not being written by people whose income depends on it. If you're willing to do this strategy well, it will make a difference.

Strategy 15: Send Bulky Mail

This is a favourite of mine. Send "big stuff`" in the envelope. If you've received mailings over the years for our Entrepreneur Summit, you know we send bulky mail. We've sent people a sand timer as we come up to the deadline for booking for the Summit. You can send people who've been customers but are no longer customers a boomerang, and on the boomerang write "I want you back." These are great examples of bulky mail.

You're generally going to do this if it's new customer acquisition with your important, strong leads. This becomes more relevant as your price goes up. It is really useful if you need to get past the gatekeeper and see people. This is a really effective business-to-business strategy.

Important to note, is that everything we're covering here is applicable to business-to-business and business-to-consumers, whether you sell products or services. It covers everybody.

A lot of people say, "I have to go into companies and get meetings, but how do I get to the decision maker?" If you want to see the chairman of a multimillion-pound company, I know somebody who used to send personalised rowing oars in the mail with a message to the CEO.

If you send the CEO of a multimillion-pound or multimillion-dollar company a rowing oar, there are two things you can be certain of. The first is he'll get the rowing oar. He'll see your business name, and it will make an impact on him. He may well follow up of his own accord. The second thing we're guaranteed of is when you make your follow-up phone call to speak to that person, they know who you are, and your chances of getting through are massively increased.

You're not going to send a rowing oar if you're selling a product for 10 or 20 pounds or dollars, but if you're doing high-end stuff, bulky mail is a really good strategy.

Strategy 16: Test Postcards

Whatever size business you have and whoever your customers are, please test postcards. Small businesses in America tend to be better at direct mail. For some reason, there's a history of small local businesses doing direct mail and doing it well. In the States, you get a lot of direct mail from your local estate agent, hairdresser, plumber, and garden store, and they're great at sending postcards.

Postcards are wonderful for a couple of reasons. Firstly, they're cheap. You don't have to pay for an envelope or pay for the envelope being stuffed.

Secondly, not only are postcards cheap, but they have a very good readership level because the person is definitely going to see it. They don't have to do anything to read it, they don't have to open anything. They're at least going to give you the chance to get your message across.

If you combine using a postcard with some of the really good copywriting and marketing strategies we use together, it's a real winner, so please test postcard marketing. You can test specific offers, events you're doing, or sales you're having. You can use postcards to sell to new customers or to do lead generation. You can use postcards to send people to your website. It's a great way to get new customers into your business.

Strategy 17: Testimonials

By now hopefully you're beginning to see you have an awful lot of options for getting more customers. This next strategy can be applied to direct mail, but it applies to all of your marketing.

You must use testimonials. They are a great way of getting more customers. There is a proportion of the population, probably 30 or 40 per cent, for whom social proof is a key element of their buying decision. Social proof is the thinking that, "Everybody else is doing this. Let's do this too."

Think of the growth of Apple's products, like the iPhone. Would it be fair to say that social proof is playing a part in its growth? If you look around you, everybody is doing this.

Everybody has an iPhone. Everybody is going to the Apple Store. Social proof is important. For a good chunk of the population, it's really important to the extent that they actually won't do business with you if there isn't some social proof.

Having real-life stories and case studies from people who've experienced and benefited from what you've got can't fail to increase your sales, so you want testimonials on your website and any written material you have. You can even include testimonials in your emails.

If you meet customers face-to-face, you actually want to have a book of testimonials ready to pull out. The time to pull them out is when the customer comes up with the objections we talked about earlier. "Your product is a bit expensive", to which you can reply "Can I show you something? Here are some people who also raised the issue of price, and here's what happened when they went ahead and did business with us. Here are their stories." Use testimonials.

Strategy 18: Video Testimonials

Obviously, to use testimonials, you have to ask for them. Please actively ask your customers for testimonials. Video testimonials are powerful and effective so it's worth going to the time and trouble to record testimonials of your customers wherever possible. If you have customers coming to wherever you are face-to-face, keep a video recorder at hand to record them, with their permission of course. If you go out to them, take one with you. If you don't have much direct contact with your customers, it's worth you or somebody going out to them and recording these messages.

You must have written testimonials, but there is an issue that people don't always believe their authenticity. That is why you need to at least have the person's name. If they work for a business, include the business they're in. Ideally, include a photo of the person. People can still be suspicious, but if they see a normal person just like them on your web page describing the experience they've had with you, it's powerful. Just doing this one thing can boost response on a sales page by 30 to 80 per cent.

Strategy 19: Direct Sales

I mentioned at the start of this book that we had micro-level strategies and big-level strategies. This strategy is one of the biggies. One of the ways to get more customers is direct sales; having a salesman or sales team go out into the real world and get sales. It's one of the obvious strategies, but everyone is very drawn to the internet and what's happening online now for all the obvious reasons and benefits. Many businesses would still benefit from having a person or people go out into the field.

One of the things that always astounds me in the documentaries on TV where trouble-shooters fix small businesses is that they find out there's normally somebody responsible for sales in some form, but nobody – including this person – actually visits people all day every day, knocks on doors, and sells stuff. It's scary, but that's the way it seems to be. Consider adding a direct sales element to your business if you don't currently have one.

Here are a few great ways of getting new customers which are rarely used but are so easy to use. I use them in my own business.

Strategy 20: Conference Calls/Teleseminars

A teleseminar or telephone seminar is just a big conference call. You book with a conference call company. You can Google "conference calls" and book a phone system, it's normally very cheap. You can have a conference call or teleseminar with 100 people, seven people, or 500 people. We sometimes have 2,000 people on these calls. They're a great way to deliver information to more than one of your customers at the same time.

If you have a small business, the nice thing is the people on the conference call don't know how many other people are on. Don't feel you need to attract huge numbers of people on the call.

Remember how our very first point was that there are people who have inquired about your business, but are currently unconverted leads? Teleseminars and conference calls work wonderfully with existing customers, but they're great for new customers as well.

All sorts of businesses can arrange a teleseminar and use it to their advantage. If you're in manufacturing, you could do a teleseminar updating customers and new potential customers on the product range that you offer. If you provide a service, like accounting, you could and should do a teleseminar a day or two after the government budget is announced to tell your customers and potential customers what's in it for them.

You can combine the customer and the new customer at the same time. You could do a teleseminar for your customers and encourage them to invite people they know. That becomes a source of referrals.

One of the things you're also going to see when implementing these 77 strategies is that once you start combining them, the sum is greater than the parts.

Strategy 21: Live Events

Before we had conference calls, teleseminars, and webinars, we'd do the same thing at a live event. This is still a great opportunity for you. It's as good for local, regional businesses as it is for nationwide businesses. A live event is where you get prospective customers into a room, and you essentially sell to them en masse by providing them with information about whatever it is you do.

An example of a business this works well in, is financial services. Let's say you sell pensions, life insurance, or investments. You put on an evening event in the town you're in, at a nice hotel meeting room somewhere, about how to retire rich. Call it something enticing like "Seven ways to retire rich when no one is able to do it."

You send out a mailing – this is great for postcards – or an email telling people about this. You say, "In this economy, people are not getting any return on their investments. They're not able to retire, let alone retire rich. Come to this free event," and they're always free, "where we'll show you seven things you must know about retiring rich." It's free, and we'll give you a cup of coffee and biscuits, whatever it may be.

You get 20, 30, 40, or 50 people into the room. For an hour, you show them how good you are at your subject. You blitz them with great tips, information, and tools. Then you present and sell your stuff. You may only convert 10 per cent of the room, but if you sell investment advice and you can get five new clients for an evening's work, that's pretty good going. Think about how you can use live events in your business.

Strategy 22: Live Online Meetings

A combination of the live event and the teleseminar is a live online meeting. If you have a wider geography, you can do the live event online in the form of a webinar or use something like GoToMeeting to do this as a live online meeting.

You can also do live online meetings one-to-one. A lot of businesses that are doing very well used to send a salesperson on a three-hour trip to meet somebody. Sometimes that's still necessary, but often they can get the same or better results by doing that meeting online. Invite the person to a video presentation online. It's an efficient way of communication, keeps costs down, and shows that you're a modern, professional business. Test this out.

Strategy 23: Conferences and Tradeshows

Could you be using conferences and tradeshows to sell more of your products and services? If you do, there's a secret. Most people pay all this money for a stand or store, stand there all day hoping and waiting, and then wonder why they don't get any sales. You want to use your stand at the conference or tradeshow as a lead generation tool. Have some kind of incentive or offer to motivate good prospective customers to do business with you. Any form of marketing needs to be eye-catching and provide some kind of reward. Tradeshows and conferences are no exception. Treat your stand as if you would any other marketing strategy. Be smart, spend some time thinking of ways to attract potential customers visually or with an offer they can't refuse, it will absolutely pay off.

Strategy 24: Banner/Display Advertising

We're going to jump back online for this one. We're going to go back and forth between offline and online because that's how you want to run your business and your marketing. It's never either/or.

Banner or display advertising is an increasingly interesting and important source of customers for all types of business, and it's emerging as very effective. It is underused by small and medium-sized businesses, which means there's a huge opportunity.

You see banner ads on the web pages you go to all the time. People say, "I don't pay any attention to the banner ads." You may think you don't pay attention to them, but generally people must do, because it's now a multibillion-dollar industry. It used to be called banner advertising, and we now tend to call it display advertising.

There are two really important things to know about display advertising that have changed radically over the last two or three years.

First is the targeting. You can target people at very specific types of websites. If you sell handbags, you can just run your banner ads to people who visit fashion-related websites or who meet the profile of your typical customers. The targeting for display banner advertising now is incredible. The other thing is, it can be really cheap. Think of the huge inventory of web pages there are. Most people are not doing this properly, so there's a huge opportunity there for you.

It would take us three days or so, to go through the ins and outs of banner and display advertising, so I'll point you in a moment to where to start this process if you're new to it. The main thing I want to convey is that it's just as easy for a small business to do this as it is for an international company. Even if you're a local business, you can just run your banner ads within 20 or 30 miles of where you are based.

If you're already doing pay-per-click advertising with Google, you do this through your Google Ads account. If you're not doing pay-per-click, you want to open a free Google Ads account with Google. You don't have to do any of the pay-per-click, but you can use your pay-per-click account for display advertising.

You go in there and start looking at the sites that run these banner and display ads. There's a website called www.20DollarBanners.com that will do your banners for you, funnily enough, for $20. You can get someone to make you these banner ads, and you can be up and running in an hour.

If you're part of any of our groups, like my VIP Inner Circle, banner and display advertising is one of the areas we focus on a lot of the time.

Strategy 25: Facebook Advertising

There are a lot of myths and nonsense spoken about social media, including Facebook. You must be careful because a lot of it is a complete waste of your time and resources.

The truth of the matter is there are very few businesses making significant money by tweeting all the time and playing around with their profile pages on Facebook. However, there is significant money being made from advertising on Facebook. You can start playing around with this for a few pounds or dollars. It's incredible.

There are two key things to understand about Facebook advertising. The first is the phenomenal reach that this has. Fifty per cent of all internet users spend an average of half an hour a day on Facebook. It's unbelievable. Personally I think it's a complete waste of time, but that's what people want to do.

If 50 per cent of all internet users spend half an hour a day on Facebook, that also means 50 per cent of your customers spend half an hour a day on Facebook. On its own, that would be significant but the real icing on the cake is that Facebook also has amazing targeting. You can find your customers without having to spend a fortune reaching everybody else.

Half your customers watch TV every day, but you can't run TV ads to reach your customers. The cost is prohibitive because you have to run ads to everybody, including people who will never be a customer of yours in a million years.

However, on Facebook, you can target people very specifically. You can target them geographically, so you can just reach people within 10, 20, 30, or 40 miles of where you are based. You can target them by age, by the relationships they're in, or whether they're male or female.

There's also a huge area where you can target them by their interests. You can target them if they're business owners, if they're into horse riding or design, or if they're fans of Coronation Street. You can target them if they've read certain books. The list goes on and on.

Here's the thing. Your customers, the people who spend money with you, have certain things in common. If you're in the wedding industry, that certain thing your customers have in common is they're getting married. You can easily find them on Facebook because there's a category for people who are engaged. Maybe you sell fashion products to people who are into certain designers, read certain magazines or books, or like certain TV shows. You can target them precisely on Facebook.

If you've not done this before, go to www.facebook.com/advertising. I should get paid for this by them, but I don't. Just start playing around, you will learn a lot just by playing around with the options you have. Maybe set up an ad and put 20 pounds or dollars in there.

Get your ads running and see what an incredible source of new potential customers this is.

For more information on how to use social media effectively to attract new customers, go to www.ChrisCardell.com for your £500 worth of FREE business building bonuses.

Strategy 26: Newspaper and Magazine Advertising

Here we are in this amazing internet world with many online choices when it comes to your marketing, customer acquisition, and business growth. There are more choices than most of us have time to deal with. That has led to people regarding traditional advertising in newspapers and magazines as almost old-fashioned. That's one issue. The second issue is that in an economic downturn, the first thing most business owners do is pull back on their marketing and advertising spend, which is a really counter-productive thing to do.

The combination of these two factors means that people aren't advertising as much in newspapers and magazines. This is a real mistake, and I would strongly encourage you to look again at the idea of newspaper and magazine advertising.

Readership is going down slightly because of the move online but there is still a huge readership for these publications.

This lack of advertising in traditional media means two things. First, the prices have gone down considerably. You can often reach people for 50 or 60 per cent of what it would have cost you three or four years ago. That can turn an underperforming ad into a profitable ad. The other really cool thing is, because a lot of business owners have pulled back, there's often less advertising in the publications, so there's less clutter. This means your message jumps out more than it would otherwise.

Bear in mind that I'm not telling you to throw huge amounts of money at any of these strategies. I am strongly encouraging you to test on a small scale. The great thing about traditional advertising is, if we can get newspaper and magazine ads to work for you, they can run month in and month out – and maybe week in and week out – for years, to bring in an ongoing stream of new customers at very little cost to you.

Strategy 27: Get More for Less

This strategy takes an interesting angle on getting more customers. You of course want to focus part of your attention on new strategies that you're not already doing. Once you're doing those marketing approaches, you want to continually focus on getting more customers from your existing marketing and advertising for the same or less cost. This isn't all just about doing new things. It's also about being much smarter about doing what you're already doing to bring in more customers.

If you run an ad in the newspaper or do a week of pay-per-click advertising and it costs you a couple hundred pounds or dollars, you're investing that money to get customers into your business. Hopefully, you're happy.

Here's the thing. You are going to spend that couple hundred whether you get five, 10, or 33 customers. Since you're investing the money, why not get really good at being able to bring in new people for the same cost?

I will give you some tips on how to do this, and these tips will apply to web pages, newspaper or magazine ads, banner ads, or direct mail. There are principles around the specific layout of how you present your offers that will apply to you.

Strategy 28: Remove Unnecessary Whitespace and Graphics

One way to get more customers for the same or less marketing cost is to remove unnecessary blank or white space and unnecessary graphics from your marketing pieces so you can get more of your sales message in.

One of our very successful members is a jewellery store. They come to our Summit and implement a lot of our stuff. In a video testimonial they've provided for us, they speak about the fact that not only are they getting a great response from their advertising, but they're pretty much the only jewellery store or retailer they know of that doesn't have pictures of their jewellery in the ads. When I heard that, I was fascinated.

They followed our advice. My advice is not "never have pictures or graphics in the ad." Most of the time, words will outperform anything else in a sales or marketing piece or an ad because you're having a direct communication with your customer.

The jewellery store has taken this to an extreme. In a very visual business, they've gotten rid of all their pictures, and they just have words. I'm not necessarily telling you to do that, but the point I'm making is don't waste space in your marketing pieces. White, blank areas, big company logos, or unnecessary graphics are a horrific waste.

That doesn't mean you can't have good, well-placed pictures or graphics of what you sell or the key people in your business. It's certainly true that photos of people will often improve response, particularly online, on Facebook, and in print advertising. You need to test this but use that space wisely. More often than not you want to use that space to convey more of your message.

Strategy 29: Make the Font Smaller

Make the font smaller so you can add more copy. The marketing industry spends millions testing all of this. The huge credit card companies, for example, do hundreds of test mailings every year with slight variations, so we know what works and what doesn't.

One of the things that's been tested extensively is reducing the font size on a mailing to put in more words. You might think that would make it harder to read, but customers will read it. Reducing the font size to get more of your message in will nearly always outperform a larger font size with fewer words.

Strategy 30: Call to Action

Make sure your ad, marketing message, or web page includes a compelling offer and a proper call to action, or "CTA". A CTA is telling people what to do. It's a really important part of any marketing piece.

We've already discussed how salespeople and entrepreneurs often don't ask for the sale, and the same is true of many marketing pieces and ads. They could be really good, but they let themselves down at the end because they don't tell people what to do next.

If you want more customers, you need to tell your potential customers precisely what to do. Tell them, "Go to this website," or "Pick up the phone and call this number." It may sound obvious. It may even sound like it's a bit too much, but it isn't. People are busy and they often need leading. They need to be told what to do.

Strategy 31: Test More Than One Way of Responding

Test more than one way of responding in your marketing pieces. The big tendency is to direct people to a web page. I'm a big proponent of that. It works well but understand that the more ways to respond you give the end user, the more responses you'll get. Yes, they can go to a web page. If they can also pick up the telephone and call you, that will increase response. If you're selling stuff in the mail and it's appropriate, they can mail things back to you. Believe it or not, there are still people who like to get things, fill them out, put them in an envelope, and put it in the post.

Not everyone prefers to visit a website, just like not everyone prefers to use the telephone. Customers are not created equal and have personal preferences just like anybody else. You may be losing out by something as simple as not having enough options for people who want to reply to you.

Strategy 32: Test Very Small Ads

This strategy is worth any and every business testing. Specifically, with newspaper and magazine advertising, try a small ad that's a couple of inches long and an inch wide that just has an enticing heading and message that sends people to a website.

The cool thing about this is that you can advertise in newspapers and magazines. If you're business-to-business, you can do it in your trade publications. You can spend a lot less on the ad to bring them to your website, and then you can use all the space on your website to convert them.

In my business I tend to send people online to a 25-minute video, by using an intriguing small ad. I don't have to take out pages and pages of ads or use pages of direct mail to get the message across. We can use the ad space really effectively this way.

Strategy 33: Pay-Per-Click Advertising

I know many business owners who have used this strategy for getting more customers and have created million-pound and million-dollar-plus businesses from nothing. Most of them have done it with pay-per-click advertising, more than anything else.

You should be doing this already, but we surveyed our customers and members and it turns out just over 50 per cent of the business owners we work with still aren't doing pay-per-click advertising, so there's a good chance you're not doing it either.

If you're not doing this, you must at least test pay-per-click advertising in your business. It is the single biggest revolution in internet marketing over the last 10 years. The main reason is that it's totally different from most other forms of marketing. Nearly all marketing and advertising involves chasing customers. You stick ads in front of them in newspapers and magazines, try to get their attention and interest, send stuff in the mail, phone them up, go to see them, and basically chase them. That's one of the realities of business, so we all have to do it to a certain extent.

Pay-per-click advertising is fundamentally different. It attracts customers without significant effort on your part, other than the effort you put time into the pay-per-click advertising in the first place, and is the only form of marketing that allows you to reach people who are looking precisely for what you have to offer.

Why chase people who may or may not be interested in what you have when people are searching Google for the product or services you sell? This applies to business-to-consumer and business-to-business selling. It applies to both products and services. If you're a local business, it's wonderful because you can do pay-per-click advertising locally, just specify the geographical area you want the ad to appear in.

If you've not tried this, please test pay-per-click advertising. If you've dabbled in it in the past and it has not produced the results you want, that may not be because it's not right for your business, it's more likely because you weren't doing some of the more advanced strategies.

Strategy 34: Obsess About Increasing Your Click-Through Rate

We've been covering the big, obvious things to get new customers, but there are so many additional elements business owners don't necessarily relate directly to bringing in the customer, and therefore bringing in more profits.

Something as apparently technical as your click-through rate on Google, which is the percentage of people who click on your ad when it appears in front of them on the page, might not seem a directly obvious way to get new customers, but, believe me, it is.

If you're new to Google, here is what happens in a nutshell. For every 100 people who are served a page with your ad, maybe two, three, or four per cent will click on the ad. The more we can get to click and the better we are at increasing your click-through rate, the more people will come to your website, and therefore the more customers you will get.

That is only half the magic of pay-per-click advertising. The real magic comes from the system Google has created. If you're new to it, or even if you're doing pay-per-click but weren't aware, Google rewards you for having a higher click-through rate by putting your ad further up the page. If you're already up there, it will reduce the amount of money you spend. When you get higher up the page, more people click on your ad, and you get this snowball effect.

Once you do your pay-per-click, you want to obsess about increasing your click-through rates. Over two, three, or four months of working on this, you can normally at least double, if not triple, your click-through rate. If you double your click-through rate, you've doubled the number of people coming into your business and increased your position on the page. You're higher on the page or you're paying less, so you're bringing in customers for a lot less money. You can use that money to bring in extra customers elsewhere. Obsess about your click-through rate.

If you are new to pay-per-click and you're not doing it yet, come back to this bit two days after you've set up your pay-per-click account, and it should make sense.

Strategy 35: Write Separate Pay-Per-Click Ads

How do you increase your click-through rate? You write separate ads all the time in your pay-per-click account. The Google AdWords system is an incredible marketing tool. It's extremely marketing-friendly and direct-response-friendly because it allows you to test different ads against each other.

You write your ad and get it up and running, and then you write a second ad to compete against the first ad. The second ad might have a different headline, use different words, or use different capitalisation, anything that might possibly increase click-through rate. We're constantly trying to beat our best-performing ad.

If you are doing pay-per-click already and you haven't tested multiple versions of all of your existing ads, you should be excited because, I promise you, there are extra customers and extra profits sitting there waiting for you whenever you do.

Strategy 36: Combine Online and Offline Marketing

This is a biggie. When the internet first came along, and even up until quite recently, people tended to regard it as a side thing. You have your business, your marketing, and your advertising. You're in the Yellow Pages, the local paper, or whatever it might be with your ads. Then there's this website thing going on, on the side and now "Oh, yeah. We have to get some traffic to our website." That is no longer a viable way to approach your internet marketing strategy. You must integrate the whole thing. If you want to be smart about it, you want to combine online and offline marketing.

There's a secret that some of the big internet marketing people don't want you to know, so I'm going to tell you. I'm privileged to know some of the world's most successful online marketers and so every now and then, about 15 or 20 of us meet for a couple of days, and we'll brainstorm what everybody is doing.

Everybody in the room is doing multi-million in terms of online selling. Everyone is obviously very good at the online stuff, like pay-per-click, Facebook, and all the rest of it. What we end up spending quite a bit of time talking about, which not everybody makes public, is how to combine traditional offline marketing with our internet marketing.

It doesn't matter how good you are at online marketing or how many great emails you send. Email open rates are 10, 20, or 30 per cent if you're lucky. That means 70 per cent or more of your customers aren't always opening your email. If we just use the internet, we're losing out big time.

The smart and wealthy internet marketers are increasingly combining online with offline marketing. By offline, I mean anything that's not online. It could be direct mail, print advertising, or getting on the phone to call people. I'm well known for what I do online, but I spend huge amounts of time working, for example, on direct mail for our business. We want to do both.

There are two principals to combining online and offline marketing. The first is to use offline media to get people online. You put ads in newspapers or send people direct mail or postcards to direct them to your website. You use offline media to put them online.

The other thing you want to do is get the online people offline. If I can get names and email addresses, I can put them on my email list and email them. I really want to get their physical address as well so I can send them stuff in the mail. I'll offer an incentive or to send something in the post, like a free DVD, to get them offline as well as online.

The more you can integrate these approaches, the more you will find that your sales increase and the more customers you will bring into your business.

Strategy 37: Use Telephone Marketing

Speaking of offline marketing and traditional marketing, there's an incredible tool that so few people use in their marketing: the telephone.

There are a proportion of your customers who are worth a lot more money than the rest. Most businesses have a chunk of really good customers, and they're probably willing to buy from you again. If you're not getting on the phone and communicating with them regularly, you're losing out big time.

It doesn't matter whether you want to personally get on the phone to people or employ somebody to do it for you. If you hate using the phone, you shouldn't force yourself to do it if you can get somebody else to do it.

When I talk about telemarketing, I'm talking about high-value phone calls, not pushing things on people. I'm talking about calling people up to have a decent conversation with them.

Let's say you employed somebody full-time who was pretty good at that. They're in your business from 9 in the morning until 5 in the afternoon, five days a week. Depending on where you are and how good they are, that could cost you anything from 25,000 to 50,000 pounds or dollars a year. Let's say it's 50,000 a year because you employ an amazing telephone person who you pay with bonuses and commissions. That is 1,000 a week or 200 a day.

This person is just calling either your good customers or the people who haven't converted yet. That's all they do all day, they don't have 10-minute breaks between each call, they're constantly on the phone. If you had that person, do you think you could bring 200 pounds or dollars back into your business? Chances are you could probably do a lot better than that, so you will want to use telephone marketing to your advantage. It's a winner.

Strategy 38: Use Phone Calls to Serve, Not to Sell

The key to using telephone marketing is to serve and not to sell. The big objection most businesses have when I talk about this is, "I don't want to pressure and pester my customers." No, you don't.

You're a customer of various businesses, both as an individual and in your own business. How many of them call you up the week after you spent money with them just to check how you're doing with what you've purchased? If they did that, wouldn't you respond positively?

If that turned into a conversation where they didn't push stuff on you but asked about what you're doing and what your needs and interests are, there's a reasonable chance you might buy from them in that phone call. If not, in the days, weeks, or months ahead you will be more predisposed to that business. You want to use the telephone as part of an overall strategy of adding strong value to your customers and potential customers.

Strategy 39: Use Deadlines

A great strategy for increasing your sales and attracting more customers is to use deadlines. There's a saying that a sales offer without a deadline isn't an offer. A deadline is a very important and powerful element of marketing.

We deliberately use a lot of deadlines in our marketing. You may have gotten this from one of our weekly offers. We offer certain products at certain prices up to a certain point. There's a clear deadline, and then it's cut off. Deadlines encourage people to act.

Here's one of the secrets about being an entrepreneur and marketing. Everyone thinks getting your customers to buy is like an on/off button where they decide to buy or not buy from you but that's simply not how it works.

The people who buy, do decide to buy from you. But it's not that the people who don't buy decide not to buy from you; it's often that they never decide. They postpone the decision, so the decision never happens.

If you understand only this, it's huge. It's not that the non-buyers say, "I don't want that." They're postponing the decision, especially if it involves spending money. If I can think about it tomorrow, next week, next month, or next year, I'm going to do it. If you can force your customers to make a decision within a certain timeframe, your sales will skyrocket.

Think of how this works in the high street. Sales have deadlines attached to them. They don't go on forever. How many ads do you see in newspapers and on TV? "It ends at 5pm on Friday." They do that because it works. It forces you to make a decision. If you know when the sale ends, you're interested in buying, and if you don't do something by 5pm on Friday, you are effectively making the decision to do nothing.

Strategy 40: Add Bonuses

Another great way to increase sales and attract more customers is to add bonuses to your offer. Hopefully, one of the things you've learned so far, is that getting customers into your business is not one-directional. There are levels of strategy, and if you work on all the levels at the same time, you will do extraordinarily well.

Some of the things we've covered so far, are at the level of finding people who don't know about you yet. If you do advertising, pay-per-lick, or direct mail, you're going out there and getting new customers. That's one level of doing things but there's a whole other level we've alluded to several times, which is increasing the percentage of the people interested in what you have, who will actually buy from you. That alone is transformative for any business.

In some businesses, 90 to 95 per cent of the people who enquire never buy, so how can we get that figure higher? If we can get those conversions higher without spending any money, it's wonderful, and one of the easier ways to do that is to add bonuses to incentivise people to buy. You can say, "I'm going to give you this product. It's £100, and I have all these bonuses to add on and give you as well."

People often laugh at infomercials, but they're worth paying attention to because it's extremely difficult to make an infomercial work. The people who do make it work put a lot of time, energy, and testing into it. If you watch carefully, one of the things they do is make the bonuses seem to be worth more than the actual product. You may have heard them say, "But wait. There's more."

Tie this in with what smart marketing is all about, which is buying customers. It's not about "Can we get this sale, and how much money can we make on the first sale?" It's about "Can we get this customer through the door in the first place so that we can sell to them for the next 100 years?" We're willing to do whatever works. So in this way It's worth adding bonuses.

If you can, add bonuses that don't cost too much money. Even if they do cost you some money, try to add some bonuses that really will incentivise and push more of your customers over the edge.

Strategy 41: Cut the Cost of Your Advertising

Let's zip back to advertising for a moment. It could be print or radio advertising, or it could be forms of internet advertising. I've already mentioned there were intangible ways of getting customers into your business. If we talk about cutting the cost of your advertising, that saves money, but how does it get more customers into your business?

It does it very directly, and here's how. Cutting the cost of your advertising can turn an underperforming ad that you're not going to bother running because it doesn't seem to be generating enough profit, into an ad you can run forever to bring in new customers.

The obvious thing we do most of the time with advertising is try to increase the response. If we can double the response to an ad, we will double our return on investment. It can be just as easy – and sometimes easier – to halve the cost of the ad. Cutting the cost of your advertising should be a big focus for you. If you've been in business for a while and you've played around with advertising that hasn't worked, chances are you are spending too much money.

Strategy 42: Buy Your Ad Space Cheaper

You can buy your advertising space cheaper by calling the salesperson just before the copy deadline. This is a really underused strategy. If you are on a sales team selling advertising at a newspaper or magazine, or even some of the internet outfits out there, you're on a bonus; you tend to get paid very high commissions which tend to be group commissions. They are normally set as monthly bonuses but it depends on the publication.

Let's say you're selling to a monthly publication or a radio station. They are going to have certain days, probably at the end of the month, when they tally up everybody's sales and dish out a bonus if you hit target, meaning everyone is trying to hit target.

Here's how to take advantage of that: Call them the day of the deadline. Call them on the last day of the month, or the day before the deadline, and say, "Here's the deal. You offered me this ad at £600. I just can't do it. It doesn't work for us. If it's of any interest whatsoever, I'll give you £300 to run this ad." If they know they're hitting target, they'll often go for it. That's a 50 per cent saving in your advertising cost.

Try to find out in your casual conversations with them when the deadline is, they'll more often than not tell you. They'll say, "I need a decision on this. The deadline is Tuesday for the next publication."

Strategy 43: Use the Recession in Your Favour

Use the economic downturn in your favour to knock down the price of ads. Especially if you're in a local business. The newspaper and magazine industries are suffering for several reasons, including the economy, but also because people are slowly migrating online.

Everybody talks about the death of newspapers and magazines. That may or may not happen but, even if it does, it's going to be a very slow one. We definitely have another five years of really good readership of print media.

Here's the way to think about it. You run your business and have your customers and potential customers who read stuff. They might read the mainstream press or the local press if you're running a local business. If you're business-to-business, they might read the trade publications. They might read unrelated stuff. For example, you may have a chunk of customers who are into horse riding and read horse magazines. Whatever it is, you want to be really focused on this migration to online as a way to reduce your ad costs.

Strategy 44: Get Someone to Buy Ad Space for You

The other way that could be worth testing is to get somebody to buy your ad space for you. These rate cards for ad spaces are basically fantasy figures used to screw money out of local businesses.

Let's take your local radio station for example. This applies to newspapers and magazines as well, but let's use radio stations. They work on two levels. They sell advertising to local companies on their rate card. They know they can get more money out of the local companies because the local companies often don't understand how media is bought. At the same time, they sell advertising to the national advertising agencies on behalf of big national companies using a completely different form of pricing, which is cost-per-thousand. It's paying for every 1,000 people you reach.

I can tell you that the national advertisers are often paying half or a third of what you're likely to be paying. If you are at the point or you get to the point where you are doing a reasonable amount of media buying of any sort, it could be well worth getting a media-buying company, advertising agency, or specifically a media buyer to do that for you, because they'll buy on a cost-per-thousand basis, and they simply will not put up with any rate card nonsense from the people you're buying from.

Strategy 45: Joint Ventures

You could do all these strategies we've covered so far very effectively for the next ten years, and you will get a lot of customers. If you and I met in ten years' time, you could tell me, "This is what we did, and we attracted 5,000 customers as a result."

But what if we could go to somebody who's already done the equivalent of that work. What if we could go to two, three, or four companies who've done the equivalent? They've put in the grind, spent the advertising money, and gotten their customers. What if we could do a joint venture with them to access those customers without having to wait.

I started off a long time ago doing marketing consulting one at a time in companies. I did a lot of traditional marketing, like direct mail, and when I look back, I actually think: "That was a bit daft."

Let's say you took everything away from me, dumped me in the centre of Britain, and said, "You need to start fresh to make your money, and all you're allowed to do is marketing consulting." Assuming nobody knew who I was, I could start knocking on doors and proving what I could do.

Or instead, I could sit down with a big or medium-sized accounting firm that had 400 small or medium-sized-business owners and say, "I can show these business owners how to make more money. If they make more money, you make more money, so everyone is happy. Introduce me to them, and I'll also give you 20 per cent of the income I get from them forever. All I need you to do is send them a letter. I'll even pay for posting the letter to them. Send them an email too." If we were in a local area, I could say, "Get them all into a room one day, and I'll do a free seminar for them." Overnight, I could get myself 20, 30, or 40 clients rather than doing all that legwork.

The question to ask if you want to pursue joint ventures is (excluding competing businesses) "who already has access to the people you want to reach?"

It's kind of crazy that retail stores don't do this more often. If I'm a hairdresser and there's a beauty salon down the street, why aren't I working with the beauty salon, swapping customers, and doing joint ventures together?

Pretty much any type of company can team up with a restaurant. The restaurant goes to the local business and says, "You have access and a good relationship with these customers. If you give them this voucher for 50 per cent savings off the next meal, I'll give you free meals at the restaurant for life," or "I'll give you a 25 per cent commission," whatever it may be.

Joint ventures do involve a bit of work however. If I went to big accounting companies, it's unlikely the first company would say, "That's a great idea. We'll do that tomorrow." I'd probably have to see five or ten of them, but then I only need one in ten to say yes.

Think of people in industries that provide things around the home, like people who sell curtains or sofas or gardening services. Why on Earth do they not have joint ventures with the local estate agents? This stuff is not complicated, it's really straightforward, but not a lot of businesses are doing it properly.

Strategy 46: Time

Joint ventures are a very tangible, obvious strategy. Let's talk about a slightly more intangible but equally important one, and that's your use of time. There's a lot going on in your life that's directly linked to the number of customers you get and the amount of money you're making, that may not seem obviously linked to the number of customers you have and the amount of money you're making.

As the owner of a business, whether you are a one-person business or a large business, chances are you play a key role in getting customers into your business. If we made a note of every single thing you do in your working week from when you get up in the morning until you go to sleep at night and then we highlighted which were playing an important role in getting more customers into your business, you would be shocked at what a small proportion of your week that is.

It is a small proportion both in terms of what you're doing, and the time spent on it. Normally, about five to 10 per cent of the business owner's week is spent on getting new customers or effective marketing. Call it marketing, advertising, or whatever you want, but it's stuff that directly relates to everything I've already covered.

It's not that the other things you're doing aren't necessary or even important. The question is whether they should be done by you. I would suggest that getting customers is the most important thing in your business.

Therefore, getting better at it is the most important thing in your business. If we could take care of that, providing you have a good product or service, everything else falls in place.

You want to be very focused on the use of your time. Unless your business is in this extraordinary place where it's already making tons of money for you, you want to start getting quite ruthless about anything using up your time that is not helping get more customers into your business.

You can't outsource this. You can't pass this buck to other people in the business. I have a lot of people working with me in various ways to get new customers into my business. My web developer, the people who run the back-office side of things, and the person who looks after the direct mail are all playing a big role in getting customers into my business. I have people who help me hands-on with marketing campaigns.

However, I don't pass on the overall responsibility for getting customers into my business. First, it's too important. Second, nobody is going to do it as well as I do. That is not because this is my subject but because, as the business owner, nobody cares more than you and me about this.

This is too important for other people to do, so start getting ruthless about using your time wisely. You want to make a really tough decision about anything you're doing in your business that doesn't involve getting new customers.

If you're going to carry on doing it, you must be pretty certain nobody else can do it or that you can't outsource it to somebody else. You may start letting things go, and they may not be done quite as well as they used to be done. That doesn't matter because you can sort that out if you start spending more time in your business. My advice as an entrepreneur is that you should spend at least 50 per cent of your time working on getting new customers into your business.

Strategy 47: The AIDA Principle

There is a core principle in all marketing for attracting more customers that works everywhere. This will work on your website, sales letters, brochures, emails, and in actual conversations with potential customers. The AIDA principle is the formula a customer goes through in their head that leads to them buying. The more you can direct that process to occur, the more money you'll make because the more sales you'll get.

AIDA stands for Attention, Interest, Desire, and Action. If I arrive at your web page, there'd better be a compelling headline that grabs my attention and keeps me reading. You need to keep my interest, or I'm gone. Interest isn't enough though. It's not enough for me to read and be interested in your newspaper or magazine ad. You need to turn the interest into a desire. Get people wanting something. You are 80 per cent there once you have the desire, but that's still not enough. There are a lot of things people want, but do they actually take action and get them? You now need to turn all that desire into action.

If you start talking to your customers about taking action and buying something from you, but you don't have their interest or desire, you've missed an important step.

If you're on the phone to a customer, or if they're physically with you and you feel that you're losing them a bit, ask yourself where you are in the AIDA process. Maybe go back to the interest point. Use this principle in all of your marketing.

Strategy 48: Free Trials

Free trials are a great way to get more customers. When two parties do business with each other, one of the two sides are taking on the risk, and it's normally the customer.

If you sell me a nice table for 500 pounds or dollars, who's taking on the risk? I am because if I give you my money and decide I really don't like the colour of the table after three days, that's tough. I bought the table. I'm taking on all the risk.

If you can reduce or eliminate the risk for your customers, sales will skyrocket. Any time you can let your customers try something out risk-free, it will have a dramatic impact on your profits.

For some businesses, that's very easy to do. For others, it's not. If you sell brand-new cars, you're probably not going to lend them the car for a couple of weeks to try it out, although I still think it would be an interesting strategy to test.

Sometimes you have to let people have the experience of an element of the business. If I'm doing complex, high-end office installations, I'm not going to install a new office on a free trial basis where, if you don't like the six months of work I've done, I'll unpack it and take it away in boxes. But if I can sit you down with an incredible 3D example of what this is going to be like for you, that's a form of a free trial.

Here's the question for you to ask. How can you give your customers and potential customers an experience of what you have to offer without them having to give you any money? The more radical you're willing to be with this, the more effective it will be.

I mentioned restaurants earlier. If I could cook, I would open a restaurant because my biggest frustration at bad marketing is that done (or not done) by restaurants.

There was a series on TV a few years ago about people starting new businesses. Two or three of them were restaurants. The basic story was these people, who were often couples or families, would give up their jobs, re-mortgage their home, and spend a quarter of a million opening and fitting out this restaurant, getting everything done, and employing staff. Then they would struggle because there were no customers.

There was nothing wrong with the restaurant or the cooking, but they had no idea when it came to marketing. They assumed that if you build a great restaurant, people will come and sit in it. That is simply not true. If you build a great website or sell a great product or service, that has nothing to do with whether people are going to buy it or not. It's all about the marketing.

If you want to open a restaurant, find an underperforming restaurant that already exists and do a deal with the owner to sort out their marketing. It will save you a quarter of a million (Send me a commission cheque if you do this).

Instead of spending £250,000, all you would have to do is allocate £3,000 to £5,000 for the following: When the restaurant opens, send an invitation to every qualified customer. This would be everybody who would potentially be a good customer, which would be anybody living in a reasonable home who has a reasonable income within your area, and you can buy lists with that on, and possibly businesses if you're doing business lunches. Send all these people lovely-looking invitations to have a free meal. You'll even throw in a glass of wine.

How much would that cost to give somebody a free meal and a glass of wine? Let's say it's £10. To get 1,000 people to try out your restaurant would cost you £10,000 of your £250,000. If you do a great job with those 1,000, you give them another voucher. When they come back to have their next meal, they get another free glass of wine. Out of the 1,000 people, you probably got 300 or 400 raving customers. Give them a referral system to bring other people. Sorted. Providing your restaurant sells decent stuff, you're done. That's all you have to do, offer a free trial.

Strategy 49: Expand Your Geography

So far, everything has been around doing what you currently do in exactly the way you currently do it but doing the marketing better. That's great, and you want to be doing all that, but next, I want to expand your thinking a little bit.

Chances are you are selling what you are selling in a limited geography. You may be a local business, and you're selling within a few miles of where you're based. You may be a regional business, and you sell within your region. You may sell nationally. You may even sell to some other countries. Whichever one of those categories you fall into, if I were to ask you if you can sell what you sell in other geographic areas, chances are the answer is yes.

If you're serving an area that has a certain population and we could double, triple, or multiply by a factor of ten the population you service or sell to, that would be a great way of bringing in more customers. What about doubling, tripling, or quadrupling the customers you bring into your business? Bear in mind, as you get better at your existing marketing, all these strategies can be rolled out as well.

One of my big messages to entrepreneurs is that wealth is a choice. The amount of money you have in your bank account is a choice. Everybody thinks the world decides how much money you've got. Well, not at the level you're playing at. Once you're a smart, marketing-savvy entrepreneur, wealth is a choice. What choices are you making about how much money you earn?

You might not want to sell to the whole country. You might not want to sell to Europe and America. That's fine, but it's a choice. Consider expanding your geography.

Strategy 50: Expand Your Products

Consider expanding your products. There's a truth about every single business out there. If we took your top 20 or 30 per cent of customers, there's almost certainly stuff they're not buying from you now that they would be willing to buy if you offered it to them.

That stuff might be directly related to your product or service, or it might be something unrelated. When I discussed joint ventures, I asked why estate agents aren't teaming up with all the other companies. It works both ways. The sofa company, the curtain company, and the gardening company are a bit daft for not teaming up with the estate agent.

The estate agent, if they were willing to effectively expand their product base, would benefit incredibly. The estate agent will tell you, "I can't expand my products because I only have one thing I sell. I sell houses, and people live in a house for eight years. There's nothing I can do." This is nonsense. The real power in your business is the relationship you have with your customers, and we're talking about leveraging that relationship. It's a very powerful thing to do.

Strategy 51: Expand Your Entrepreneurial Horizons

If you want to get really into this, expand your entrepreneurial horizons. When you made the decision to go into the business you're currently in, you probably didn't know what you now know about marketing. If you're on a path of learning, certainly you're going to know more in three months, six months, a year, or two years down the line.

If you were to go back to the point where you set up a business in the first place, if you knew then what you know now, would you pick that business? Would you pick that business and other businesses? Would you pick totally different businesses? A lot of serial entrepreneurs become very wealthy. Remember that you always have the choice to do more and to do different things with the skill that you have.

I gave you a strategy for making any restaurant profitable. I talked about doing that with a new restaurant. You could equally do that with an existing restaurant. If you are ever strapped for cash, all you have to do is bang on the door of ten restaurants that are serving decent food but haven't got any customers and repeat the strategy.

As an entrepreneur, you can now apply your marketing skills in all sorts of arenas. You could do it with your existing business or your new business, and/or you could team up with others to do it. The world is your oyster.

I'm not encouraging you to open 23 businesses if that's not your thing. I spend most of my time turning down offers to do extra stuff because I'm very focused on what I want to do with my time. I don't want to get into the loop a lot of successful entrepreneurs get into, which is that they just can't say no. What I'm talking about is the theme here, to reach more customers. Has it crossed your mind that one of the ways to do that is to reach customers from totally unrelated businesses? It's an interesting thought.

Strategy 52: Test Permission Marketing

Permission marketing, rather than marketing that sells to people straightaway, is marketing that gets a customer's permission to begin a relationship with them. It is a fundamentally different form of marketing than most marketing, but it plays a big part in what I do and what a lot of our business owners that we work with do.

In a lot of arenas, it's too much to ask people who don't know you to spend money with you. The classic example is a website. If someone who didn't know you two minutes ago arrives at your website, the chances of you getting money out of them are slim. Specifically, less than 1 per cent of people who visit a typical website will buy from that website.

If you use a permission marketing model, you can say to visitors to your website, "You didn't know me 30 seconds ago, but I have some really interesting, some useful information. I've put it on a free online video for you. Just give me your name and email address, and here it is." Instead of a 1 per cent response, you'll probably get a 15 or 20 per cent response rate, maybe even higher.

Permission marketing is great because then the customer watches your video, they're really into you, and they probably will contact you anyway. If they don't, you've got their email address, and you can follow up with them.

Strategy 53: Measure and Test Your Marketing

Testing is the foundation of all marketing. It directly relates to getting more customers into your business. The basic principle is you want to test all your marketing. First, you want to test new marketing methods, like some of the ones I've been offering you here. I'm not promising every single one of these will be wonderful for you. I am promising that if you're willing to test and find out which ones are, some of them will be game-changers.

Finding out that something doesn't work is really important and useful. It's just as important as finding out what does work.

When we do any form of marketing, like the pay-per-click ads, we want to test different ads to improve the response. Any form of testing that improves the result of your marketing brings you more customers. If you're running a successful ad in a newspaper or magazine, test it with a completely different headline. If that gives you a 15 per cent increase in customers, there you go. You must measure and test all of your marketing.

Strategy 54: The 80/20 Principle and Profiling

This is a more advanced strategy, but you definitely want to do this. You want to attract new customers into your business, and you want to do it fast. If you want to be successful and wealthy, you don't want to spend all your time thinking, "How can I get more customers?" You want to ask, "How can I get more really good customers?" It's a different level of thinking.

The 80/20 principle applies in virtually every business. We find that about 20 per cent of your customers generate about 80 per cent of your profits. There are all sorts of reasons for this. We don't need to go into them here, but it's a very standard rule. It can vary a bit, maybe it's 70/30 or 85/15, but the point is it's never evenly proportionate to the effort you put in. Not all your customers are worth the same to you. There's a chunk of your customers who are worth more, normally a lot more.

Let's suppose you acquired 1,000 customers over time, and of those 1,000 customers, 80 per cent of the profits in your business only came from 20 per cent of them. We can go out there and get another 1,000 customers, which is great because that would double the size of your business, but what if the next 1,000 customers all came from the same category of that 20 per cent? I can't even do the maths on what that would do to your business. It would be incredible.

In the back of your mind as you implement all these strategies, you also want to think about how to get not just new customers, but the best new customers.

As far as you can, start profiling your customers. First, identify the groups spending the most money with you. See what patterns and commonalities there are. They'll possibly be in a certain age group or in certain types of businesses. If you sell to consumers, there may be bias toward male or female. Maybe women are your best customers. There may be a bias to certain geographical areas or toward income levels. You may do better with wealthier people.

You want to know all this so that when you do your marketing, you can target people, and there are two ways to do this.

You can do this informally yourself if you're a smaller business. Think about the customers, talk to them, look at their lives, and find out what's going on. If necessary, survey them. Send them an email to one of those online survey systems.

If you have a larger business, you can do this professionally through a company. We did this process last year. You give the company all your customer information, including how much these customers have spent. They do whatever they do with their computers and numbers, and they come back with a report showing that your best customer is in this age group, this social group, or lives in these kinds of areas. Then we can go back with our marketing and target the right people.

If you have a decent customer list and you want to do that, the company we use is called Blue Sheep, www.bluesheep.com.

Strategy 55: Guarantees

I mentioned guarantees when we talked about risk elimination. If you want more customers, guarantee what you sell. It's as simple and straightforward as that. You should have strong, compelling guarantees throughout all your marketing and advertising. People understand this logically, but they're not always doing it.

If somebody spends money with you and they absolutely hate what you do for them, chances are you'll probably give them a refund or partial refund, depending on what you're selling. Given that's the case, you want to be explicit about that. You want to make it a core part of your marketing message. On your website and marketing material, guarantees should be everywhere. Trust is important, and it sells.

Strategy 56: Sell Benefits, Not Features

Make sure all your marketing is talking about the benefits and not the features. This is one of the fundamental marketing mistakes that people still make, and they make it a great deal.

If I want to buy a new Hi-Fi and the salespeople start telling me about how many decibel levels are coming out of the woofer and the speaker, and that it took 19 hours to make in Taiwan, then, unless I'm a complete Hi-Fi geek, I really couldn't care less. They're just listing me the features, not the benefits. The benefits are that this is going to look lovely in my home. It's going to produce amazing sound. I'm going to listen to stuff, and it's going to feel like I'm in a concert venue where it's taking place.

You need to know what is important to your customer. Some people will buy a Hi-Fi because it will impress the neighbours. If that's your customer's thing, you need to hammer home on that. You want to sell benefits and not features.

If you're selling hammers, you're not selling a hammer or even the hole in the wall; you're selling the ability to put an amazing picture, photo, or painting on the wall and give that person a wonderful experience every time they look at it. You need to apply this. Look at all your marketing, particularly things like the home page of your website. You need to start telling your customers about the benefits within the first one or two sentences.

Strategy 57: Networking

When you talk to business owners, one of the things that always happens is they stop doing the stuff they did at the beginning that was really successful for them. It's sort of understandable because you end up busy doing 101 other things. Sometimes it can be so easy to radically change what's going on in the business.

In the early days of a business, most business owners have to sell their wares wherever they can. You want to be out there interacting and networking with fellow human beings as much as you can. It is one of the most obvious but underused ways to get more customers.

This is going to depend on what you sell. If you sell to consumers, where are the consumers? Where can you hang out with them? If you sell to businesses, where can you hang out at business breakfasts or whatever it might be? Do things really well when it comes to networking or mixing.

The internet is wonderful. We tend to think we can achieve all this online. Obviously, we now have social networking sites. Many people will say Facebook is the equivalent of traditional networking, but it's not. That's complete nonsense when it comes to owning a business because you do not have the influence you would have over another human being when you are looking at them face-to-face and networking with them.

Strategy 58: Public Speaking

Other than one-to-one or face-to-face selling, there is no better way to influence people, let people see what you have, and sell, than speaking to a group of people, especially in the early growing days of a business. If you can get within 100 miles of a group of people who will listen to you for an hour or two about what you have to offer, you really should be doing it. It can be a big boost early in the business's growth, and it only costs you your time to do.

A lot of people don't like the idea of public speaking because it scares them, but the key to public speaking is getting up, being yourself, and just communicating to people. I used to do this in the earlier days of my business. I spoke to a small group of business owners in Sussex. I remember I did an hour-and-a-half talk, and there was some interest. A couple of them later did some bits and pieces with us.

Last year, I got an email from one of the people who was in the audience of that group. They had just become a customer of ours and started spending money with us. That evening had made an impact on them. It works.

The other thing about speaking to groups, is that you are then perceived as an authority.

If you can possibly get in front of any group that includes potential customers of yours and give them useful and interesting information, whether you are business-to-business or business-to-consumer, please consider doing it.

Public speaking is a good thing to do. It's also a very good skill to hone because you never know when it will come in handy.

Strategy 59: Public Relations

I've already covered a bit on advertising and spending money on advertising, and it's well worth you doing that. But before we go spending a fortune on advertising, how about getting advertising for free in the form of free PR, or public relations. It's a great open book sitting there for business owners.

There's a core principle for you to understand about PR. Everybody thinks it's difficult to get into the media, but actually the opposite is the case. I used to work in media. I used to work in radio, so I know exactly how it works.

In any newspaper or magazine or on any radio or TV station, there are producers or journalists almost pulling their hair out because they have to fill hours of radio or TV time or pages in newspapers and magazines. They have to fill it with interesting people and interviews, and that's hard to find.

For example, when you're looking to fill a radio show that has some speech content on it, not only have you got to find a subject that's interesting and somebody who knows what they're talking about, but that person has to be able to communicate and be somewhat eloquent.

There are things you know about; either the type of business you're in, the product you sell, or the arena you work in that segments of the population out there are also interested in. Providing you're able to meet the needs of the producer or journalist on the other end, you will find they are far more receptive than you might think to giving you PR coverage.

Let's talk about some specifics on how to do that.

Strategy 60: The "5 Top Tips" Press Release

This is a real PR secret for you that is simple and straightforward. Whenever I'm advising somebody on getting started with PR, I tell them to try the "5 Top Tips" press release strategy. This hardly ever fails.

There's something you're an expert on. Let's say you're an accountant, and it's budget time. You could go to your local media with five top tips for cutting your taxes, saving for retirement, or retiring early. If you sell office supplies, you could go to the local media, to certain business-to-business publications, or to the business section of The Sunday Times and say, "Here's a great story for you. How about the five top tips on creating the perfect productive and relaxing workspace?" Put all this into a press release and come up with your five top tips.

Why does this work so well? Think about what I said about these producers and journalists. They're looking for a good story. The five top tips thing is literally handing them their story on a plate. They will write an article or produce a radio feature around these five top tips. It's also really useful for you because when you get on the media or if you're interviewed, you have your five bullet points to talk about. The "5 Top Tips" press release works really well.

Strategy 61: News Story Association PR

Another strategy to try is the news story association PR. This means you piggyback on the back of stories in the news.

Have you noticed that when there are stories in the news, the media try to interview people about the stories? One of the things local television news does particularly well, and to a certain extent radio and local newspapers, is to find what's called a local angle to a national story.

You can apply this to any type of business, but we were previously talking about the annual budget as an example. After the annual budget, you'll find if you watch your local TV news channel, they interview local business owners to find out what they think about it. There's no reason you couldn't piggyback on that story and tell them you're available for interview. Fax or email them a press release or call them up to tell them that you're available.

Another type of story to watch out for is celebrity stories. Let's say you are involved in the fashion industry. When there's a big celebrity event and all the celebs are out in their finery, you could contact magazines or your local radio station and position yourself as an expert in fashion to come onto the station as a guest. The opportunities are endless.

Strategy 62: Local Radio PR

If you want a specific step-by-step strategy for getting PR coverage and getting the ball rolling, one of my favourites is local radio PR. Particularly if you're in Britain but really wherever you are, you're going to have local, regional radio. This works particularly well in the UK because every region has a BBC local radio station. One of the rules is that these local radio stations need a percentage of the broadcasts to be speech content. They can't play records 24 hours a day. They have to talk about stuff.

That's tough for the producers because it means, yet again, they've got to fill the shows. Unlike the national media where they can get famous people in, all they've got on the local media is local people, so they are desperate for local guests.

If you want a little strategy, combine a couple of the things we've been talking about. Do a "5 Top Tips" press release or look out for a national story that you can hook yourself into, and contact your local radio station. If you're in the UK, find out the names of the shows during the day and contact the producer of the morning show on your local BBC radio station. If they're not interested, contact the producer of the afternoon show because they're different people doing a different thing.

If you do this, six to seven times out of ten, you will get on that station providing you're able to talk. You don't have to be a gifted speaker. They'll be listening on the phone just to make sure you're clear and eloquent, so prepare beforehand. Do your five top tips or do five or six bullet points so you've got something clear and concise to talk about.

PR is wonderful because it's free advertising, and it also helps build your credibility. It helps establish you in that leadership position.

The next two methods for attracting customers are related to your pricing and how people pay.

Strategy 63: Premium Pricing

Everybody tends to assume that putting your prices up or selling more expensive stuff can have a detrimental effect on your ability to get more customers. That's not always the case. There is a segment of the population reluctant to spend money on products or services that appear too cheap. This applies more to the wealthier and affluent buyer.

Regardless of what you're selling, you will find that a very interesting approach which very few people use, is to target your customers accurately, so you need to know who your customers are. For those who have the ability and any sign of willingness to pay for more expensive products and services, make sure you have a premium-priced version to sell to these people.

By premium pricing, I mean a more expensive and more high-end version. If you sell shoes, and your average shoe is £50, make sure you have a £500 or £600 option in there. You won't lose anything because if you keep the lower-priced option, you'll keep the customers you get that way. The addition of a premium-priced option can actually bring you in new and more customers who you would not have reached in the first place.

If I'm looking for a product or service or someone to help me with a certain area in my business, I'm going to think twice if it's too cheap. Suppose I want the world's greatest search engine optimiser to work on my business. If I hear recommendations, and finally find somebody who tells me their rate is $10 an hour, I will question whether they're good enough to do what I want doing because shouldn't they be charging more than that?

The whole area of pricing is fascinating because when you set your prices higher and move to a more high-end business, it helps convey a completely new level of doing business. Premium pricing can be a customer acquisition strategy, and very few people understand that.

Strategy 64: Payment Plans

If you are able and willing to give your customers the option to pay in monthly instalments, you will normally see an increase in sales in at least the 20 to 40 per cent range. If you normally have a one-off payment and you let customers pay over two or three months, that will normally give you a significant increase in sales, depending on where you are priced at the moment. If you sell particularly high-end expensive products or services, you can extend that to even longer.

Just splitting a payment into two or three changes the perception because the customer will be very focused on that monthly payment amount, rather than the total amount. Making higher priced products and services more affordable, without reducing your costs is a very effective strategy.

Strategy 65: Radio Advertising

Radio advertising can be a great part of the marketing mix, particularly for a growing business and particularly if you have a strong local or regional presence. There are lots of businesses who created themselves off the back of good radio advertising. If you're a national business, it's something to test doing nationally.

You need to be careful because it's easy to spend a lot of money, and you don't want to do that without getting any return. It's certainly worth doing low-cost tests on the radio, especially if you are a local or regional business. Local radio reaches a good percentage of the population. If it's done right and you're not paying over the odds, it can be a worthwhile strategy.

Going back to one of our earlier points, you may want to get people doing your media buying for you and this applies to radio too. If you buy radio advertising on the rate cards these radio stations try to offer, you'll be paying far too much money.

Radio advertising is something to test, but please follow our golden rule: You must test and measure all your advertising. Radio advertising, like all marketing, is well worth testing.

Strategy 66: Use Your Contact List

Using your contact list is a strategy that's overlooked. You and the people in your business have a network of people in your phone books or mobile phones, and that is your contact list. Within that contact list, you have people who might become customers or people with access to potential customers.

When I talk about your contact list, I encourage you to look at yourself, your life, and your history, and all the people you've ever had contact and good relations with.

One of the things that most successful, wealthy entrepreneurs are very good at is tapping in to the people they know or the people who know the people they know, even if some of those links are tentative. If we have a relationship with somebody or a relationship with somebody through somebody else and we're asked a favour, most of the time we will do it.

If you're trying to get access to a certain type of business, a specific person in a business, or certain types of people to reach as customers, take a good strong look at your contact list. There are people you could contact if you needed to, either personally or by phone, email, Facebook, or whatever it is. Ask yourself who in that list could be a customer or potential customer.

The network marketing industry, which I am not a huge fan of, is a big industry that makes a lot of money. It doesn't always make a lot of money for most of the people in it, but that's a story for another day. One of the ways they do this is to convince the new member, the new person selling their vitamins, health products, or whatever it may be to tap in to their network of people. In some cases, it works.

We're going to do all this more advanced marketing and advertising, but isn't it a bit silly to not first tap into your own existing contact list? Have a think about that and focus on areas or people within that list that you can tap into. Think of colleagues of colleagues or friends of friends. If you know someone whose sister is in that industry, go for it. Being an entrepreneur, you have to push the boat a little bit and sometimes go a little bit beyond your comfort zone. This is important because it doesn't matter how great your product or service is, if nobody knows about it or buys it, it's all about getting more customers.

Strategy 67: Niche

Niching is such a great source of potential new customers. It involves something fundamental about how people buy. People will be more inclined to buy from a company that is more focused on their specific needs.

Suppose you needed heart surgery. You had a choice of two good surgeons. All Surgeon 1 does is the particular heart surgery you need. It's complicated, but they do it every day. In fact, they've done it for the last ten years day in and day out, and they can do it with their eyes closed. Surgeon 2 is an equally good surgeon, maybe an even better surgeon, with an outstanding reputation. Surgeon 2 has a gift that they can do hearts, legs, knees, brains, and anything at all. Every couple of weeks, they'll do heart surgery, and every now and then they'll do the type of surgery you need.

Which surgeon would you pick? You're probably going to pick the first one because they have gone into a niche. So as consumers or buyers, we are more inclined toward that niche.

This is something to start thinking about within your business. It doesn't mean you have to stop or change what you're doing necessarily, but you may want to introduce elements of your business that are just for that niche.

Financial advisors can advise on mortgages or insurance, and maybe they work on helping business owners get loans. They have that skill and ability. If I was doing the marketing for one of those businesses, the first thing I would do is divide them up. I would have them as separate entities, possibly with separate names and certainly with separate websites.

If you are looking for insurance as a business owner, the website you end up at is a website just about insurance for business owners. It's not also about mortgages and this, that, and the other. There's no great logical reason to that because there's no reason somebody can't multitask, but we're just more comfortable. Your sales will increase if you target a niche.

If you fix cars for a living, and you move into a new city where you set up a garage fixing cars, one of your challenges is you're the new person, and there are 27 other garages in town. Why on Earth should they come to you? If you're willing to be the person who focuses on just fixing BMWs and you set up a BMW-fixing garage, you narrow your market, but it makes the sales message to that customer so much easier. It also makes the customer easy to find. All you have to do is market to BMW owners, and you can get mailing lists of BMW owners.

How could you niche in your business? How you do this is up to you, but it makes the marketing a lot easier if you can just go for specific people and reach certain people within that arena. Niching is an effective strategy for customer acquisition.

Strategy 68: Online Video

When online video started taking off, it was this cool thing you could add to your website if you wanted to. Online video is now a central part of your online marketing strategy. I can tell you, through extensive testing, it makes a direct impact on getting customers into your business.

You must use online video in the right place and test it because there can still be times when a page of copy will outperform a page with a video on it, but overall, online video will increase sales.

If you look at how the internet is moving and developing, websites as we've known them up to now are starting to phase out. The thing we refer to as the internet is becoming more of a multimedia environment. The boundary between your internet experience and your television experience is starting to disappear. It's all starting to merge together. Five years from now, a business's website won't feel like a website. It will feel almost like a mini TV channel or certainly a mini multimedia experience.

Online video works because it taps in to the brain's conditioning to respond to things on television. Of all the forms of advertising – newspapers, radio, and TV – television has always been the most expensive because it's perceived to have more impact. That's partly because it's multichannel, so you're seeing and hearing, but more because it has an authority to it that tends to have a bigger impact. Using that same principal in an online strategy on your website will normally have a significant impact on sales.

If you're sending people to your website, a percentage of those visitors will convert to buyers and adding the right online video is going to make a difference to your conversion rate.

Strategy 69: Remarketing

Remarketing is proving one of the most effective and powerful internet marketing methods for attracting more customers into your business. When somebody visits your web page but doesn't buy from you or give you any contact details, until now you've had no way of following up with them. If they're one of the 99 per cent of website visitors who go to a site and just move on without buying, normally we've lost them and can't follow up with them.

Remarketing solves that problem. When somebody comes to your website, a cookie is placed on their computer. Then remarketing banner ads, banner advertising, is served up to that person for days, weeks, or months ahead. On Google, you can do it up to a year and a half after they've visited your website.

You can do remarketing at a very advanced and sophisticated level and it is worth studying remarketing in detail. On a very basic level, you can do this in your Google Ads account. You just set up a separate campaign using their remarketing system. If you haven't got my programmes on remarketing, you can just search within Google. There are some help videos that show you how to do set it up.

It's very simple. You or your web person puts a little bit of code on your web page and from then on, you will be able to serve up banner and display ads to those same people. What we're doing here is stacking the deck in our favour. We're piling on various methods on top of each other to increase your ability to attract new customers. Remarketing is a very effective way of compounding your marketing efforts.

Strategy 70: Bundling

You can bundle the products you offer together to create packages, to increase sales. If I owned a camera shop selling digital camera stuff, I could measure how many people buy from me. Maybe one out of ten spends on average £70 or £80 on a camera. I could try not changing anything that's already working, but additionally have a bundled option. If they want, they could get the camera in a bundle, with a tripod and a lovely full colour book with 101 photography tips for just £99.

Bundling works because it greatly increases the perceived value. Suddenly, I'm not just getting a camera. I'm getting the camera, the tripod, and the book. Combined, that has a reasonably good perceived value for only £10 or £20 more than the customer was paying for the camera.

If you do this properly, it's not going to cost you much more. You may not even make additional profits per sale. In other words, you might give them the tripod and the book at cost price, but what if that gets two people out of ten instead of one person out of ten who come into the shop to buy from you?

Consider how you can bundle. You can do this with services too, we're not just talking about physical products. When a free service warranty is added onto a product, that is a form of bundling. When postage, packing, and shipping is added on free to a product, that is a form of bundling.

Have a look at that. That shift in the perception of that first product can really make a difference to your sales so it's well worth testing.

Strategy 71: Reshape Your Core Product or Service

Unless you're a huge retailer or online retailer, most businesses have one, two, or maybe three main products or services the new customer buys, even if you have a range of stuff you sell them down the road. In a lot of businesses, there's one thing you sell at one level, and that's what you do. Reshaping or changing either the amount, quantity, or quality of that first offering can have very interesting consequences on sales. You're basically changing the offer.

When we test any new marketing method – an ad, internet advert, or something on a website – we can test the copy, headlines, or price. One of the first things we want to test is the actual offer. Customers will respond very differently to small, discreet shifts and changes in that core product in ways that are very hard to predict.

We do a lot of testing in my business because we focus a lot on getting new customers. It's obviously important to us, as it is with any business. We normally do a compelling offer for new customers, and we do lot of testing. Would they like a DVD or CD, a six-DVD pack or a multi-CD and DVD pack, or a booklet, report, or eBook? We do a lot of testing and changing of the core thing we offer as our front-door product, if you will, the first thing people get.

Whenever you test this, you tend to see very different responses to different types of products and different price points. It's almost impossible for you as the business owner to be the best judge of what that should be because you're too close to your business. It's worth testing and trying that out, so play around with this. Step into the shoes of a new customer. Have a look at what you're offering them as the first thing to buy. Test variations on that.

You can test a bigger, more expensive thing. That can be very interesting to do because sometimes you can get an increase in price without losing your sales rate, which is great because it's giving you more money immediately. Sometimes a reduction in price will double, triple, or quadruple those early sales. Remember, we're buying customers. We're bringing customers in through the door. Reshaping your core product or service is a good way to get sales.

We've done some advanced strategies, and now I'm going to give you a really advanced one. Virtually nobody does this, but if you are willing enough, smart enough, and persistent enough to do this, this is a brilliant strategy for getting customers.

Strategy 72: Other Businesses' Non-Buyers

This seems counterintuitive, which is why so few people are willing to do it. You say to your competitors, "We're competitors, and that's fine. Think about this for a minute. You spend money on marketing and advertising. You have a website and all the rest of it. Some people contact you but don't become customers. You've spent good money trying to get those people, you've basically paid for non-buyers. I'm in the same position. My non-buyers aren't going to buy from me, and yours aren't going to buy from you. How about we make some money out of this and give each other access to the non-buyers?"

Sometimes people just won't buy from you for whatever reason, but we know they had an interest in the product or service. Maybe you just weren't right for them. If someone different comes along with a different offering, it's a really cool strategy. It's a little bit like joint ventures. You'll immediately get access to people who are that close to becoming customers, and you're not losing because you're giving the competitor access to people who probably aren't going to buy from you anyway.

To pull this off, you need some tenacity. You need to be persistent because most of the competitors all say no to doing it. If you can have a decent conversation with them, it's an interesting one to pursue.

Watch the huge multibillion-pound or multibillion-dollar companies, particularly in the tech world. Apple, Microsoft, Google, and Facebook all compete with each other at certain levels, yet they tend to have simultaneous cooperative relationships.

Apple and Microsoft are direct competitors in some areas. There are even those Apple ads where they took the mickey out of the Microsoft geeky users. They are direct competitors. If you look back in time, you'll find some Apple ads that Bill Gates appeared on because they also have a relationship. Microsoft works on software for Apple, and they have this ongoing continuing relationship.

The top brass, the owners, the founders of those companies understood that they were playing a bigger, more important game than just being at each other's throats all the time. They're still competitive and they still fight for market in some areas, but they are smart enough to cooperate with others. Don't rule out cooperating with your competition. Normally the pie is big enough for everybody. It's worth considering this for your own business and can be a really good strategy if you are willing to try it.

Strategy 73: Become an Authority – Claim the Leadership Position

As you go through these strategies, there are a couple of things that will make a difference to all of them working well.

When you use direct mail, do something online, or have online video, there are certain layers you can add that will help each of them improve significantly. One of them is the extent to which you or your business is regarded as an authority in the marketplace. You want to claim the leadership position because in any type of business or arena, there is a leader.

If I say "fizzy cola drink," you probably think Coca-Cola. If you're in Britain and I say "a really famous hypnotist," you probably think of Paul McKenna. There are other cola drinks out there, and there are thousands of hypnotists, but Paul McKenna and Coca-Cola have established themselves in the leadership position.

I mention Paul specifically because I know him. We worked together on a radio station a long time ago before I was doing this and before he was doing what he now does. I know for a fact that he decided to establish that leadership position and started pushing himself forward as a leader in that field before he'd done all the things that would naturally have him labelled as a leader. He understood either intuitively or he learned that if you wait for somebody to label you as leader, often you will have a very long wait.

Some of our members and customers have done very well. When I go to their websites, I smile because I see the phrase "Britain's leading wedding photographer" or "Europe's leading manufacturer of screwdrivers" or "America's leading real estate," whatever it may be. They've claimed that leadership position.

If you're willing to be bold – and you do need to have a bit of boldness as an entrepreneur – you want to claim that. Someone is going to claim it in your industry if they haven't already. Why not you? That will have a direct impact on attracting customers.

You must back that up, but I'm giving you all the strategies here to do it. For example, your use of online video can back up your leadership position because you're online as an expert and an authority. Getting PR coverage and appearing on your local radio station is going to back up your leadership position.

Hopefully one of the things you're seeing here is the sum of these is much greater than the parts. Any one, two, three, or ten of these strategies are great. If you start doing them all, they have a huge knock-on effect for your business.

Strategy 74: Become an Authority – Write A Book

Another way to become an authority, which I recommend everybody thinks about, is to write a book. The first reaction people have is, "I'm in a very mundane industry. Why would I write a book?" I'm not talking about writing a book to get on the bestseller list necessarily. That's fine if you want to do it. The truth of the matter is, most non-fiction books have a very low readership level. I'm talking about writing a book purely to give you that authority position.

Write a book or get a ghost-writer to write a book with you on the areas in your business that you're an expert on. They could be technical areas or mass-market areas, it depends entirely on you. Most people have specific knowledge that has value to other people. Put that in a book.

Even if you self-publish and print 1,000 of them, the purpose is not to get into a bookstore. The purpose is to have your customers see you're an author of a book, which gives you instant credibility. Secondly, you can use that book as a marketing tool. You'll often see smart marketers giving away books as a free gift on their website or in their ads.

Writing a book is wonderful because it has several immediate impacts. It helps credibility and authority, but it's also a great early sales or lead generation tool. Give it some thought. You're here because you want more customers. If you do it, you will get more customers.

Everybody can write a book. You may actually have a book inside you that somebody will publish. Just so you know, if you can be pretty sure that 4,000 to 6,000 people will buy your non-fiction book, you'll probably get somebody to publish it. That's not seen as at all bad. If not, just write your own and publish it yourself. It's not a significantly huge investment.

Strategy 75: Action and Implementation

This is the foundation on which everything is built. Hopefully, you understand that you have more than enough strategies now to get as many customers as you want. Why wouldn't you go out there and get them? The only reason that you would not succeed at this, is by not acting and not obsessing about implementation.

If you're smart enough and determined enough to still be reading this far, please don't let yourself down by not taking action, by not implementing these marketing strategies in your business. This is all about implementation. You don't have to be a great or experienced marketer; you just need to be willing to take action, and more action than anybody else.

Remember the importance of this subject here. You're not actually here because all you want is more customers. You're not even really here because all you want is more customers to help the company grow.

The truth of the matter is you're a business owner. As a business owner, everything financially in your life, the financial wellbeing of yourself and maybe your family, and the property you own, all depends on your ability to get customers.

I hope you're inspired and excited at the opportunity here. Please do something with that excitement and inspiration. Take action.

We have two strategies to go. The first one is an important psychological mindset strategy. The final one is a very specific strategy that will make you oodles of money. I've saved one of the best until last.

Strategy 76: Understand the Real Business You're In

If I was to say to you before today, "What business are you in?" or you came to a seminar and asked everybody in the room one by one, "What business are you in?" you'd probably get 200 different answers from the 200 different people in the room. "I'm in the wedding industry", "I'm in the manufacturing business", "I'm an internet web designer." But that's not the real business that you're in.

The real business you're in is marketing. The real business you're in as an entrepreneur is getting customers. Unfortunately, we take for granted the quality of the product or service we provide. Obviously, that needs to be in place, but that's like getting up in the morning. It has to happen anyway. That's not the real business you're in, or what will determine your success or failure, or the level of success you experience. The thing that will determine your success is how many customers you get, and the thing that's going to determine how many customers you get is your marketing.

The real business you are in is marketing, so you should start every day focusing on that. This loops back to one of our earlier points when we looked at time. I would reinforce the message that the amount of time you are willing to spend on marketing is a vital part of all of this because that's the business you're in.

Let me give you a really cool strategy to round off with. This is so simple, straightforward, and obvious. It is the real untapped profits that sit in every business, but virtually nobody does it.

Strategy 77: Reactivate Old/Lost Customers

If we want to give a business an instant cash boost, we start talking to the existing customers because they're so much easier to sell to than new customers. Everybody focuses on that group, and then the second group are the non-customers, and they're much harder to get to buy.

There are actually three groups. In between the existing customers and the non-customers is the group of your old customers who are not buying from you anymore. They are customers who are still there in the mix but have stopped buying from you or you stopped offering them stuff, or they're lost customers in the sense that they were customers of yours once, and they're not customers of yours anymore. They've gone away, and they're spending money with somebody else. You have a great opportunity to reactivate both of those categories of ex-customer.

If you have a new business and are not in this position yet, please make a big note of this because this is going to be one you absolutely want to implement. Reactivating customers who aren't spending money with you, for whatever reason, is one of the real delights of marketing because everyone is pleasantly surprised about this.

Understand that if people have stopped spending money with you, it rarely has anything to do with you, apart from the fact that maybe you're not communicating with them enough. It is rarely because they can't stand you or whatever it may be. There may be a few of them in the mix, and obviously you have to let some people go if they're unhappy. That's fine.

Generally speaking, people stop buying from a business because the business ignores them. It is quite likely you've ignored people who have spent money with you three months ago, three years ago, or maybe even longer. If you're willing to reactivate them, you'll be pleasantly surprised at how many come back.

The second chunk of these people are doing business with and therefore spending money with other people. For whatever reason, they stopped doing business with you. Everybody thinks you can't get those people back, but nothing could be further from the truth.

Think about your own life, there have been businesses with which you've spent money. I'm not talking about people who do a horrific job for you, but businesses you spend money with, and there were okay but not great, or they didn't follow up with you, so you now spend your money with somebody else.

It's rarely the case that the somebody else you're spending money with is the greatest thing since sliced bread, so here's what you need to think about. These former customers of yours who are now spending money elsewhere, are probably just as frustrated with the "elsewhere" product or service as maybe they once were with yours.

Here's how you deal with the former customers or the lost customers. You're very honest, open, and upfront with them. You write them a letter or send them an email, but I think direct mail is better for this. If you sell at a higher price point, do this personally. Do it on the phone or arrange to go see them. Say to them whatever you need to say to honestly get them back.

If you've not paid enough attention to them, apologise. Say, "I've been thinking about it, and I don't think I've paid enough attention to you. I haven't contacted you over the last few months. I've not been checking how you are. I just want to check in with you. How are things going? Is there anything I can do for you?"

If you think you've lost them to somebody else, one of the great marketing letters goes along these lines. "Dear Julie," or "Dear John, was it something I said? Was it something I did? I'm shocked and mortified that I may have upset or offended you. If I have, I deeply apologise.

"I value your business, and I miss you. If I've done something to let you down, I would really like to know what that is so I can put it right. If it's just that time has gone by and we haven't been in contact, I'd like to re-establish our relationship and let you know how important you are to me. I'm just checking in to see how you're doing."

When did anybody last say that or anything similar to you? It doesn't happen, does it? Like all the strategies we've talked about here today, it's simple and straightforward. It can be profoundly profitable, but virtually nobody does it.

Whether you're self-employed, an up-and-coming entrepreneur, the owner of a small, medium, or large business, I have a simple message for you: wealth is a choice.

It's really down to you now on the number of these 77 strategies you are willing to implement.

Bear in mind that if you tried one every week, then in a year and a half, you'd have 77 new approaches to your business and your business will be absolutely transformed.

Thank you for spending this time with me and for investing this time in yourself. I appreciate that you stuck through this because we covered a lot of material. I would love to hear your success stories, so please do get in touch with us.

Good luck with it all. Take massive action and reap the rewards.

For more strategies, tips and tools on how to grow your business and get more customers, go to www.ChrisCardell.com for your £500 worth of FREE business building bonuses.